FOR BETTER OR
VERSE

BY GEORGE, HE DID IT!
175 LIMERICKS

GEORGE R. ROBERTS

 FriesenPress

Suite 300 - 990 Fort St
Victoria, BC, V8V 3K2
Canada

www.friesenpress.com

ISBN
978-1-4602-9731-5 (Hardcover)
978-1-4602-9732-2 (Paperback)
978-1-4602-9733-9 (eBook)

1.HUMOR, FORM, LIMERICKS & VERSE

Distributed to the trade by The Ingram Book Company

Enjoy

G Roberts

BY GEORGE, HE DID IT!

First impressions are important.

Limericks are fun oriented. In case you're not familiar with their origin you can blame them on
The Emerald Isle. They are defined as: "a poem of five lines named years ago after Limerick, a town in Ireland ,where the locals met in the pub and created indecent, in a humorous sense, poems.

But who is this man, George R. Roberts? I'm a fun kind of guy. I even am, at some risk, a punster.
To put bread on the table I'm a chartered accountant but to enjoy life my real passion is music.
Because she was of Scottish birth my wife called me Geordie, in Mexico I'm Jorge and I won't tell you what my mother called me. Well, I will: it's Ratcliffe. That's my middle initial. Straight out of Burnley, England.

In the music world I was choir leader for over 40 years in local churches. Singing got me to the Louise
Rose Good News Choir – 350 voices 80% females – good odds. We even had female tenors who needed a shoulder to lean upon. That's when my love of limericks started. In 1997 at choir practice

the first half hour of rehearsals was spent showing off our newly created limericks. Music and poetry were a fit.

Proceeds of the sale of this book are being donated to the Foster Parents Plan. The Plan has received my support since 1985. George says thank you to Friesen Press for their encouragement and easy access during the printing process. Also special thanks to Anne Jarvis for suggesting the limericks be put into a book and for her priceless – which means she doesn't get paid – help along the way.

George R. Roberts

Table of Contents

This nonsense costs but a few bucks;
You can't really say the price sucks.
As you read each verse
(They get worse and worse)
Just make your aim good - Geordie ducks.

CHAPTER ONE
BUSINESS

It's really none of yours ...

There once was a man they called Andy;
Folks called him because he was handy.
He had all the tools
And he knew all the rules.
Too bad that our Andy was randy.

We enjoyed his fine wit and his candour
And knew that he liked to philander.
The women he dated
Were highly x-rated,
This eye guy named Doc Alexander.

We sent her to see a new doc,
A big, handsome guy and a jock.
He gave her his hand
And they walked in the sand;
Her heart became sound as a rock.

George R. Roberts

There once was a surgeon named Denis,
Who enjoyed all the sports, such as tennis.
He would cut through your jaw
With a dirty, old saw;
His nickname was Denis the Menace!

I went to a dentist named Erin
Who bloodied the smock she was wearin'.
To tell you the truth,
It all came from a tooth
While Geordie was cussin' and swearin'.

*Often business acquaintances become personal friends.
It's considered a no-no to mix business and pleasure,
but John is the exception that proves the rule. He didn't
object (too much) to seeing his name in print.*

John T. is a building contractor
And into each job he must factor:
The time that he's working,
The coffee he's perking,
The cost of his brand new Ford tractor.

To try and do things on the cheap,
He raises some horses and sheep.
You have to believe
The stuff that they leave
Helps pay for their board and their keep.

John T. has a passion for dogs
He takes them along when he jogs.
According to Chris [his wife]
"Don't you believe this!
My John in spandex? The mind bogs."

When John built our lovely sundeck,
We paid him by cash, not by cheque.
They caught him for fraud
and he said, "Oh, my God!"
The fine was ten years in Quebec …

George R. Roberts

The name "Thomas" shows that he's Welsh
But when he tries singing, you squelch.
I laughed till I cried
And his wife nearly died;
The best he could do was a *belchhh* …

She goes by the name of Sher-lee;
Her job is a snap actual-lee.
From nine until four,
She just sits by the door
And grabs all the patients' mon-nee.

The teller was simply called Bill;
He kept not his hand from the till.
The bank had no clue
Just how much he withdrew
Until they probated his will.

The name of my chiro is Wayne;
I went there because I had pain.
"It's all in your head,"
That is what the man said;
I'll never go back there again.

We all know a taxman named Lou,
Who smiled as he tightened the screw.
His victims were wise
For they told him no lies
Because the false statements were true.

I once worked for Revenue Can.
They trained me to be a taxman.
But I must confess
I'm no Elliot Ness—
The first sign of trouble? I ran.

George R. Roberts

He laughed when they sent him to jail;
He cried when they told him, "No bail."
When things were all sorted,
He hadn't reported
A two million dollar land sale!

My wife goes to see Dr. Walker;
Doc listens 'cause she's quite a talker.
He's not a head-shrinker
Her back he did tinker—
The poor girl fell off of her rocker.

They called the receptionist Bert-a;
With all the men patients she'd flirt-a.
When guys were in trouble,
Our Bert booked them double.
She cared not how much it might hurt-a.

"Chiropractor" is not just a word;
They manipulate things, so I've heard.
I also should mention
Away goes your tension.
By twisting your spine? That's absurd!

She married a guy known as Brian
On whom all the lake was relyin'
To provide them with jokes
About simpler folks
To forget how much gas they were buyin'.

She brought me this year's income tax.
I told her, "Go home. Just relax!
The little you make?
No time it will take
To do the whole thing on my fax."

CHAPTER TWO
CHOIR

It seems to me I've heard that song before ...

In December 1996, Louise Rose placed an ad in the local paper for singers to join a choir she was forming (no audition) based on her background as pianist, singer and composer—350 singers showed up. Limericks were born …!

Anita lived far out to sea;
New husband and daughter made three.
How deep is the ocean?!
The kids had no notion
Their lives were in such jeopardy.

George Frederick Handel was great;
We all know his music was straight.
His once famous chorus
Does nothing but bore us
Because it is so out of date.

Good Friday comes just once a year
At which time we all shed a tear.
But do not despair;
Are you not aware?
That's when our new choir will appear! *[Easter, 1997]*

Tuesday's practice cannot come too soon
Like *Der Bingle* we try to croon.
We work through each measure;
Good ones we will treasure
For concerts in April and June.

The tenors that sit in our row *[mostly females]*
Do nothing but get up and go.
If you're in row five,
It's just like a beehive.
(I sit there so that's how I know.)

The hall has a single latrine.
With three hundred singers—I mean …
Some drank up their water;
They shouldn't have oughter,
Like Vita and Al and Eileen.

Our leader's eyes are such a treat;
They laugh when we don't get the beat.
She leads on the chorus
While sitting before us
And pounding the floor with her feet.

Whenever I'm feeling quite blue,
I just put a call through to Sue.
"First you smarten up
Then go have some sup.
That's what a cor Limey would do."

We sit where we want in the choir
And trust in the Lord to inspire.
He makes us sound swell [that word?]
But Satan says, "Hell!
I'd better go stoke up the fire."

Three hundred singers were in place;
How many could our leader face?
They tested her cool
But she's nobody's fool—
The altos were all singing bass.

When I was a lad, I was shy
But now I'm a pain in the eye.
And every chorus
Of *Wee deoch-an-Doris*
Goes down with a smidgeon of rye.

The parking lot fills up real fast
And nobody wants to be last.
The biggest by far
Is the pianist's car,
A tank from the far distant past.

There's not many choirs like ours
That practice one page for two hours.
The reason? Miss Rose
Keeps holding her nose—
We come straight from work (so no showers!).

If music is really your thing
Then come out to practice and sing.
Just check the agenda
Naught ought to offend ya;
You'll yodel with Bach and with Bing.

The choir decided to hold a dance at McMorran's (local dance hall) and the Dal Richards band came over from Vancouver.

Do you have a yearning to dance
And maybe your life to enhance?
The Dal Richards band
Will give you a hand
And May twenty-two is your chance.

Perhaps you have nothing to wear
For the fun night-out dancing affair.
Just go incognito
And rent a tuxedo
Or shrug "I don't care" and go bare.

I went to the dance with Louise
Despite my arthritic old knees.
We sure had a ball,
Though I can't quite recall
Why the cop ordered, "Follow me, please."

What they do now really ain't dancin';
It's more like two elephants prancin'.
They don't swing and sway
In the old-fashioned way—
Now there's not much chance for romancin'.

You know that I hardly can wait
To go on our big dancing date
But with my angina
A slow boat to China
Would be the best thing for my fate.

Will you ever forget our wee Pat?
She was known as a swingin' hep cat.
Pat went out each night
Till dawn's early light
Then sat with the milkman to chat.

When Mitch (Miller) took our leader to lunch,
I'd say (though it's only a hunch)
That he made her day
When she heard him say,
"You amaze me girl—quite a bunch!"

By the way, the choir, formed in 1997, is still in biz!

George R. Roberts

Our leader likes her flowers floral *[what else?]*
The colour she loves best is coral.
A rose would be swell
And we'll never tell
That shade is just slightly amoral.

What gets up my butt? It's the basses!
They cannot be holding four aces.
This tenor finds strange
By singing their range—
Puts smiles on everyone's faces.

Melinda is known best as Mel;
She sings in the chorus quite well.
She's cute and she's sweet
From her head to her feet.
If only more stories she'd tell.

The choir called her "Simple Pat."
She wore an unusual hat.
The thing kept on squirmin';
It couldn't be ermine—
Her cat simply captured a rat.

I quite often think about Pat,
Who liked to hold hands and to chat.
But I blew my chances
With my sly advances;
She hit me ... and that ended that.

(Are you sick of Pat yet?)

Have you heard of the girl they call Pat?
She's the one that sings notes that are flat
When she sees the sharp signs,
She avoids those land mines;
Our dear Patsy's as blind as a bat.

George R. Roberts

CHAPTER THREE
FAMILY AND USED-TO-BE FRIENDS

You can pick your friends but not ...

There once was a lady called Verne,
Who caused all her friends some concern.
She fell out of bed
Right onto her head
And had what is called a "slow burn."

Zena was asked to play cello;
She plays it quite well and it's mellow.
But to her disgust
They said that she must
Not perform till they'd served all the jello.

Kenya worked in the garden quite late
But he wanted to meet with his mate.
When he heard Big Ben chime
He was off like a dime
'Cause he knows that his Tracey won't wait.

George R. Roberts

There once was a lady named Kay,
Who wanted to shop at The Bay.
The cab that she hired
Broke down and expired;
I can't print what Kay had to say.

My neighbour's a man known as Gerry;
The things that he tells me are scary.
His life is a blast
But who could forecast
His scooter would slip off the ferry.

There once was a lady named Joyce,
Who had quite a soft little voice.
She did her good deeds
By hoeing out weeds;
On Sunday she chose to rejoice.

She went by the name of Doreen;
To organize things was her scene.
While others might play
She would spend night and day
"Get with it!" (you know what I mean).

I know that my wife was averse
To seeing me eyeing that nurse.
So Kate said, "That's great
If you go have a date.
You'll learn about Better or Verse."

There once was a girl known as Kate,
Who blossomed in life rather late.
She had her first date
At age eighty-eight—
One wonders what she used for bait.

My two favourite girls, I confess,
Are Terry and her daughter Jess.
Their poem's super
Only one boo-boo
(The thing doesn't rhyme—did you guess?)

*Which reminds me of what the organist said after I'd shown
him an arrangement I'd done of Dvorak's Goin' Home—"The
author won't mind; he was already decomposed."*

To all the cute girls in my life,
I tell you I still love my wife.
I can't hurt her feelings
With clandestine dealings.
(She'd find a new use for the knife!)

There once was a girl they called Deb
Whose spirits would flow, then would ebb.
She spent her free time
Knee-deep in some crime
Like watching some hunk on the web.

There once was a girl known as Nora
Who didn't know fauna from flora.
She lacked expertise
Re: the birds and the bees ...
Then how come she knew-a the score-a?

There once was a lady called Anne,
Who went to Cancun for a tan.
The sun of a beach
Turned her white to dark peach,
Then Dole sealed her up in a can.

There once was a lady called Anne *[again?!]*
Who loved to perform with a fan.
Her routine was flawless
And then she went braless—
Our cute lady Anne was a man!

There once was a man they called Brian
Who asked his wife, "Cook me Hawaiian?"
She did what he said
Till they found him quite dead;
Her tears were from laughter, not cryin' …

It wasn't as if she did plan it;
She came from a different planet.
She'd fingers and toes
But no human nose;
Then how could she pick it? Poor Janet!

Favourite dance? It's the one o'clock jump.
Favourite actor? I'd say Andy Gump.
And my favourite drink?
Geordie can't even think—
Been drunk since the stock market slump.

Ken drives a big bus and he's cool;
Survives thanks to one golden rule.
Young kids and old elders
Punks, winos and welders,
His secret? Counts ten … he's no fool!

There once was a lady called Bea,
Who had a tattoo on her knee.
The men were impressed
When Bea got undressed
And there was so much more to see.

There was a young fella called Ted,
Who believed all the things people said.
It was not surprising
He panicked when rising—
His wife had just shouted, "Drop dead!"

There once was a young man named Ray,
Who couldn't hold onto his pay.
He ended up broke
And it wasn't a joke;
He gave all his money away.

The girls in the store called her Bette,
The one with her hair in a net.
I heard what they said,
"Today she is red.
Tomorrow who knows what we'll get?"

There once was a girl, name of Liz,
Who went through her life in a tizz.
Spent all day in bed
And it's there that she said,
"Get lost 'cause it's none of your biz!"

My wife's cousin, monikered Frances,
Reads only those red-hot romances.
Fran goes to a mystic
Who is altruistic—
Puts into perspective Fran's chances.

She was known to her family as Gail.
She could ski, she could swim, she could sail.
Her consorts were legion;
They came from each region.
Thank God Microsoft has email.

Larry said he would like to teach school
So he studied quite hard, like a mule.
He got his diploma
From old Casa Loma *[in Toronto]*
In Latin it read: April Fool!

George R. Roberts

You know Dr. T. was my hero;
He told me to go see Doc Nero.
"With skill he will measure
Systolic blood pressure.
Let's hope that it's higher than zero!"

The mall has a special drug annex
Where George goes to purchase his Xanax.
He's hale and he's hearty,
The life of the party,
Until he forgets and he panics!

There once was a girl they called Nada
Who did only things that were bad-a.
She was so beguiling
She left the guys smiling;
It's her man for whom I feel sad-a.

There once was a guy they called Tony;
He was the real thing—not a phony.
What made the girls vanish?
He spoke only Spanish
And spent all his time with a crony.

*On the occasion of friends planning to
return to the USA …*

Oh, why's their life so full of stress?
They will be missed, I do confess.
They are on their way
Back to U.S. of A.
Brian, Terry and their daughter Jess.

There once was a young girl called Terry
Who liked to have fun and be merry.
But when she got hitched
Then she bitched and she bitched *[not really]*
Poor Brian lost all of his hair-y.

Of course what I write is not true
But what can a bystander do?
When all through the years
The song that he hears *[their favourite jingle]*
Is all about love being blue …

CHAPTER FOUR

FEMALES

No man is going to tell me what to do! ...

In the chapters about males and females, the victims are a mix of real and fictional. One example is Azula—she's real. Keep reading. You might be in print. Females are listed in alphabetical order.

It's hard to pronounce her name, Aase [Oh-Saw]
There's nothing that comes even close-a.
Between you and me,
The family tree
Has roots in far off Nova Scotia.

Her friends would all say: Oh, that's Ann!
She keeps herself cool with a fan.
And just for a treat,
She will moisten her feet
By sitting all day on the can.

"There once was a girl named Azula
Who spent overnight in the cool-a
She tried to sing blues
And drank too much booze
She only could sing "boolah, boolah".

There once was a girl known as Bert;
At Abbeyfield her job was dirt. *[Abbeyfield House]*
She was trim, she was neat,
She was fast on her feet
And with the old men she would flirt.

There once was a girl known as Bev;
She married a preacher called Rev.
They made quite a pair
That's until her affair
Then Rev told her, "Go to the Dev–"

Our club had a swimmer named Clare,
Who dove in the pool without care.
She would have been fine
If she'd read that large sign:
"The pool is now closed for repair."

Dianne is in charge of our care;
To do that, she always will stare.
We fixed her one day
When we went out to play
In only our old underwear.

You knew when you saw them both sit
That Doris and Nora would fit.
They'd grab the same key
From the B down to C
And play everyone's favourite hit.

When Elizabeth Squance was first born,
She looked sad and a little forlorn.
But now she looks great
And is quick to relate
She's married to Alan Haythorne.

George R. Roberts

There once was a lady called Ellie,
Who danced up a storm with her belly.
She did such contortions
(In epic proportions!)
Like nothing you'd see on the telly.

There once was a girl they called Floris,
The prettiest thing in the chorus.
When she sang and she danced
All us guys were entranced;
We never let Floris ignore us.

There once was a baby called Fran;
She was born, then both parents ran.
Her mom and her dad
Knew that they'd been had;
She sure wasn't part of the plan.

"Amazing" was what they called Grace;
She brought her squeeze-box just in case.
She'd play any old tune
For as long as we'd croon—
A credit to God's human race.

When she asked me if I'd like a date,
I thought, "Wow! That's really great!
We can go to a show."
So it came as a blow—
She'd referred to the kind that you ate.

I remember a girl we called Jen;
She had lots of style, do you ken?
Her guys went astray
And still, till this day,
Her nightly prayers say: "Ah … men …"

There once was a girl they called Jess,
Who Friday night had to confess.
She'd married in haste
And, oh, what a waste,
The cost of her new wedding dress.

The lim'ricks draw nigh Roman "C";
That's one hundred verses, you see.
You can't stop them coming
'Cause my brain keeps humming;
My head's buzzing 'round like a bee.

There once was a lady called Joan,
Who lived by herself all alone.
Along came this gent
With cunning intent;
The moss never grew on her stone.

There once was a girl named Johanna,
Who thought she could sing high soprano.
She sang really high
As she sailed through the sky
Having slipped on a slice of banana.

There once was a girl named Louise
Whose dogs gave her all of their fleas.
She told them "Beware
With whom what you share
You'll end up in Mommy's deep freeze."

There once was a girl known as Mary;
She grew up quite fast on the prairie.
It wasn't the stubble
That gave her the trouble—
It was the farmhands at the dairy.

George R. Roberts

Mary Ann has a "dish" who's her twin;
They ride at the drop of a pin.
But get in their way
And choice words they will say,
Bringing meaning to blasphemous sin.

I thought you should hear about Millie,
Who's quite an exceptional filly.
She's a girl, not a horse
So I'm filled with remorse
'Cause to shoot my poor bookie was silly.

There once was a lady called Nora,
Who loved nature's fauna and flora.
She also loved Brian
Who always was sighin',
"You keep such a wide open door-a." *[soirées]*

Alaska is where lives my Pat;
Patricia's at home with her cat.
They both like to jog
And live high on the hog.
(And you don't believe half of that!)

She's known as our Peppermint Patti,
The one who puts cream on her latté.
Her expensive couture
Costs a fortune, for sure,
The view of her rear drives men batty. *[a friend in Alaska]*

There once was a girl they called Sonia,
Who loved to cook things like lasagna.
She sent her friends cards
That expressed her regards
With beautiful words like "good on ya!"

There once was a girl they called Sue
Whose doctor said, "You've got the flu."
Sue said, "You're just crazy!
And don't be so lazy
Are aspirins the best you can do?!"

There was a sweet thing, name of Susan,
Who straight for a bruisin' was cruisin'.
Her long list of "others"
Had very strict mothers
Who found her lifestyle not amusin'.

I think what our Terry abhors
Is that no one stays home to do chores.
With time to reflect,
What did she expect?
They all love to be out of doors.

CHAPTER FIVE
MALES

He who wears the pants, I think …

There once was a guy they called Adam,
Who tried to resist a young madam.
She looked in his eyes
As he ogled her thighs
And smiled—'cause she knew that she had 'im.

There's one thing I'll say about Brian
On whom the whole team was relyin'.
The guy had a passion
For taking a bashin'.
He gets an A-plus just for tryin'.

There once was a sailor named Frank;
They told him to go walk the plank.
With tears in his eyes
He said bye to the guys,
"Just make a note of where I sank."

There once was a fella named George,
Who thought he could be Victor Borge.
Though he worked like a dog,
Really all he could log
Was a one-nighter down at the Gorge. *[a hotel in Victoria]*

There once was a singer called Grant,
Who sang with a group that could chant.
They all had a ball
Driving friends up the wall;
He wanted to quit but he can't.

There once was a Scotsman called Keith;
They found his knife still in its sheath.
Although he was tight
And put up a good fight,
The damn thing was stuck underneath.

We all knew this fella called Ivan,
Who took a wee course in sea divin'.
He dove to the bottom
And that's where they got him;
His course should have been in "survivin'."

There once was a young man named Jack,
Who ended up flat on his back.
The reason he fell
Was quite easy to tell—
The guy had a burger attack.

Rob's happy as happy can be;
He lives with his wife by the sea.
If they had one wish
T'would be to catch fish
Then all they could eat would be free.

George R. Roberts

She married a fellow named Ted;
They lived all their life in the red.
He was a nice guy
So she didn't know why
She smiled when her Teddy dropped dead.

These five lines were writ by a man
While sitting one night on the can.
His thoughts were so deep
That he soon fell asleep
And no one knew where he began.

CHAPTER SIX
MISCELLANEOUS POTPOURRI

It nearly rhymes with Mussolini …

"Potpourri" is defined as a mixture of dried petals and spices placed in a bowl to perfume a room, or (as in this case) there was no other place, we assume.

Life doesn't care what you wear
Or what things you might do to your hair.
If it's true love you seek
Try not to be meek;
To earn happiness, two must share.

I hope that this stuff will soon end
Me-thinks he has gone 'round the bend.
It's verse after verse
And each one just gets worse—
You pick a good place and we'll send.

We come to Mt. Newton for care *[a day centre]*
To see all our friends who are there.
They bring us by bus
Without any fuss
And don't give a damn what we wear.

The world was a simpler place
When TV was not in our face.
We'd go for a walk
Or just have us a talk
Instead of our present rat race.

If poets use words like "befall"
Old Webster will have to install
A new set of rules
To cover the jewels
That songwriters use like "Y'all!"

My parents came over from Britain;
With Canada, they were soon smitten.
They progenied me
And as you can see,
George likes to make rhymes that are written.

Music transcends racial woes
As inward the harmony flows.
Like sweets in a bowl
It can touch every soul.
How come? I'd say, "Nobody knows."

Real love is a thing to remember
As life moves on through to December.
The memory of Love
Is a gift from above;
The fire ignites from an ember.

I eat peanut butter each noon
To keep the old muscles in tune.
Then add some banana
I'm off to Nirvana (never heard of it)
A (dill) pickle takes me to the moon!
(try it - you'll like it)

I played with my own special deck
You cheated? I said, "What the heck."
The name of the game
Is not to proclaim
When the croupier writes out the cheque.

To those who try hard but then fail
To keep out of long terms in jail,
There's a lesson to learn
And it's how to discern
Which friends'll come up with the bail.

When Clayton and Karen got wed,
Their friends and their relatives said,
"The light of the day
Will not shine their way
As they spend all their time in their bed."

CHAPTER SEVEN

NATURE

This isn't about the birds and the bees ...

The dictionary describes "nature" as the world with all its features and living things. Living lakeside for over forty years gave us an opportunity to communicate with all types of birds. Our love of dogs meant there was always a canine around as part of the family.

I told my dog, Sooze, "There's a hitch;
Your dad just found out you're a bitch.
They say it's no thrill
To be on the pill
You go with the flow or you switch."

We took our dog Sooze to the vet,
Which triggered a stream like a jet.
She "went" in the car
And then won a cigar
For all the new places she'd wet.

I laughed as I came out with Sooze;
It looked like she couldn't hold booze
But the shot in the bum
Was sedation, not rum—
She just needs to have a good snooze.

Sooze, by the way, was really called "Susan."

Sometimes when my old dog would bark,
I'd drive him along to the park.
He'd have ecstasies
When he saw all the trees;
We'd never get home until dark.

A blue heron stopped on our lot;
It's not like it shouldn't have ought.
It walked with such grace
Then left not a trace
Of all the good things that it'd caught.

It's well worth the price of admission
To watch a blue heron go fishin'.
You just have to wait
Till the neck goes out straight;
New meaning is brought to attrition.

Though I thought I should talk to the deer,
They said, "Get the h--- out of here!
We pay for our food
(And to put it quite crude)
By depositing dung from our rear."

They say that things happen in threes
Well, except for the birds and the bees
'Cause they do it in tandem
Quite often at random
In water, on land and in trees.

There once was a male they called Drake,
Who was known to his kin as a rake.
He said "I'm a mallard.
See, my Doctor Ballard
Sells animal food, heaven's sake."

"Quite a bitch" is what people called Peg
As the brown fur she wore showed some leg
And her eyes hypnotized
All the gals and the guys
Every time she sat up just to beg.

There once was a lab cross called Susie,
Who acted the part of a floozie.
Though boy dogs were smelling,
One dog was repelling.
(Our Susie, the floozie, was choosey).

When Pedro brought Belle to the door,
We wondered what next was in store.
Poor Belle was a wreck;
Kate said, "What the heck,
We've plenty of love for one more."

*Belle was our name for her—later, we found her real
owners, who'd strangely named her "Elizabeth."*

CHAPTER EIGHT

POLITICS

Too bad about the Reform Party ...

Bill Clinton lives up on the hill
And where there's a way there's a will.
He cultivates aides
Of various shades
Then Congress gets stuck with the bill.

The gen'ral was known just as Ike
Like the Dutchman who plugged up the dyke.
But kidding aside,
His skill stopped the tide;
The enemy all took a hike.

The card he was dealt made him jump;
His hand is so strong he could bump!
But here in the West,
The gamblers know best—
The joker this time could be trump.

The boss of the House was Pierre,
A man with political flair.
To London he went
With cunning intent;
No longer the Queen do we share.

From out of the West came Steve Harper,
Who proved he was very much sharper
Than those in the East
On whom he did feast;
He used a red pen as his marker.

This man really liked his cigar;
Through smoke, Churchill won us the war.
Though beginnings were small,
We all heeded his call
And the enemy wanted no more.

There's a man who would not get my vote,
Yet, he really is worthy of note.
With his peccadilloes
On various pillows,
It's his wife who ends up as the goat.

George R. Roberts

CHAPTER NINE

RELIGION

I never thought they would be open ...

The head of the ushers is Neil,
Who was chosen for his sex appeal.
Then a gal named Joan
Was heard to groan,
"He's my husband. There's no big deal!"

There once was a Baptist named John,
Who got up so early he'd yawn.
He preached every day
Till he heard people say,
"You know, John, my sins are all gone."

The Bible transcribes as great prose
A good book, which everyone knows.
But who did the writing
That is so exciting?
Some little old monks on their toes.

There once was a lady named Sue,
Who locked herself in the church loo.
She ranted and raved
And she begged to be saved—
So now she is one of the few.

There once was a pastor named Ron
On whom, one might say, the sun shone.
They missed him one Sunday;
It wasn't till Monday
They found him asleep on the john.

It's clear what the good Bible said:
"Be careful whom you take to bed.
If you live in sin,
You will be done in."
So Dave and Bathsheba got wed.

If limericks bore you to death,
Recall what the Bible has saith:
"Don't do adultery
Unless she is sultry,
Then go to the priest and confessth."

Her boyfriend showed up at the church;
She phoned up and cancelled the search.
'Cause what she did carry
Meant that they should marry;
She thought she'd been left in the lurch.

I wondered—would there be seating
At the church's annual meeting?
With plenty of room
It still seemed like a tomb
Till do-gooders all did their bleating.

George R. Roberts

A teacher at church named Charmaine
In charge of the children's domain,
As one of her tools,
She threw out the rules
And then ran like h--- from the blame.

Galina was found through an ad;
The previous guy had been sad.
She brought lots of class *[an organist]*
To liturgical mass
Plus smiles that she always had had …

There once was a girl called Ginette,
As Catholic as you'd ever met.
On coming to Grace *[Lutheran]*
She did about face
In order to cover her bet.

The trouble with Kyla? She flirts!
I mean you can see through her skirts.
Along came this guy *[same religion]*
With a very good eye;
They married … and soon had two squirts.

Try singing it to "Blest Be the Tie That Binds."

CHAPTER TEN

SPORTS

Oh to be a jock in Scotland! ...

To quote a Canadian sports announcer commenting on the cool displayed by the Canadian women's curling team: "Ice water melts and comes through the windows of their souls."

They cried as their flag was unfurled,
A tribute to how they had curled.
Five girls from the West
Turned out as the best,
The best of the rest of the world.

I curl all the time so I know
The best way to throw rocks is slow.
I can't comprehend
How the team blanks an end
When into the lead they would go.

Nagano was very low key;
The Japanese said it would be.
With smiles on their features,
They watched from the bleachers
As everything worked to a tee.

I'm sure there are others competing,
If so, their appearance is fleeting.
Canada and the U.S.
The world? They could care less
As long as home teams did the beating.

Two teams were gung-ho to play hockey;
Thought they would win gold in a walkey.
But as play did unfold
The bronze, silver and gold
Were won by the teams not so cocky.

The Blue Jays win games every day
No matter which teams they do play.
Home runs are their style;
They hit them a mile.
(I still think they get too much pay!)

That's 174. There's one more!
It's been fun doing this, not a chore.
I had a good time
Making rhythm and rhyme …
What's that in the background—a snore?!

CPSIA information can be obtained
at www.ICGtesting.com
Printed in the USA
LVOW12s2246240317

528435LV00001B/36/P

9 781460 297322